High Speed Tractor

A VISUAL HISTORY OF THE U.S. ARMY'S TRACKED ARTILLERY PRIME MOVERS

By David Doyle
and Pat Stansell

Ampersand Publishing
COMPANY, INC.

Published by Ampersand Publishing Company, Inc.
235 N.E. 6th Avenue, Delray Beach, Florida 33483
Tel: (561) 266-9686 • Fax: (561) 266-9786
www.ampersandpublishing.comf

Credits: Many of the photographs displayed in this book were obtained at the National Archives and Records Administration facility at College Park, Maryland (NARA II). This facility contains millions and millions of images documenting the rich visual history of the United States of America. Other images were obtained from the U.S. Army, Aberdeen Proving Ground (APG), The Library of Virginia and the Patton Museum, Ft. Knox, KY. Still other images were obtained from private archives and archivists who preserve these unique records at their own expense. Special thanks go to the John Adams-Graf Collection, the George C. Marshall Museum, Overloon, Netherlands, Deere & Company Archives and the LaPorte County Historical Society. Wright Patterson M2 photos and research assistance by Michael Kalbfleisch. Uncredited photos are copyright of the authors.

Cover: The photo of the M6 on the cover was shot by John Adams-Graf and the vehicle belongs to the George C. Marshall Museum, Overloon, Netherlands. **Title page:** *A new M6 sits in the yard of the Engineering Standards Vehicle Laboratory in Detroit, Michigan in late 1944.* **Back Cover:** M5 high-speed tractor shot by John Adams-Graf.

Agent in the UK: Historex Agents, Wellington House, 157 Snargate Street, Dover, KENT CT17 9BZ Tel: 01304 206720 Fax: 01304 204528. E-mail: sales@historex-agents.com

Agent in Italy and Europe: tuttostoria, via G.S. Sonnino, 34-43100 Parma, Italy Tel: 39-0521-292733 Fax: 39-0521-290387.

Agent in Hong Kong: Falcon Supplies Co., 201 Chit Lee Commercial Building, 30 Shaukiwan Road, Hong Kong Tel: 852 2886 2290 Fax: 852 2886 3001. E-mail: falcon@hk-hobby.com.hk

Agent in Japan and the Far East: HobbyLink Japan, Tatebayashi-shi, Nishitakane-cho 43-6, Gunma 374-0075, Japan. Fax: 81-276-80-3067. E-mail: dealers@hlj.com

Table of Contents

High Speed Tractor development 3

M2 High Speed Tractor 5

M4 High Speed Tractor 26

M5 High Speed Tractor 51

M6 High Speed Tractor 77

M8 High Speed Tractor 101

Introduction

Among the greatest assets of the U.S. military during WWII were their highly mobile artillery units. U.S. artillery was almost totally mechanized, ranging from Gun and Howitzer Motor Carriages (self-propelled artillery in today's nomenclature) to artillery towed with wheeled prime movers, which, depending upon the piece, could be anything from a Jeep to the huge Mack NO 7 1/2-ton prime mover. Between these extremes were the high-speed tractors.

When it comes to tractors, the military's idea of "high speed" doesn't mean freeway speeds. Rather it serves to distinguish these vehicles from the "normal" crawler tractors—similar to bulldozers that had been used as artillery prime movers prior to this, and briefly continued in use alongside the high-speed tractors.

During WWII, three families of these vehicles were designed from the ground up for this purpose, the M4 18-ton, the M5 13-ton and the massive M6 38-ton tractor. A forth high-speed tractor, the M2, was a 7-ton rated vehicle that was used predominately around Army Air Force airfields, although they were occasionally used in the field, as well.

The bulk of the photographs for this book were taken at the Engineering Standards Vehicle Laboratory. The Engineering Standards Vehicle Laboratory was located near the Office of the Chief of Ordnance in Detroit. At the ESVL, various vehicles were studied by Ordnance engineers and draftsmen when making design changes, or to calculate loading and shipping data. Practically every type of ordnance vehicle or vehicle-related equipment passed through this laboratory. Design changes could be prototyped and installed on vehicles at this facility to check for fit, clearances, etc. Extensive photographic records were made. It is these photos that have been drawn on to illustrate the "as-new" status of these tractors.

G-096 M2 High speed tractor

The smallest high-speed tractor in the Army's inventory was the M2 7-ton high-speed tractor developed by the Cleveland Tractor Company (Cletrac). These vehicles were also produced by John Deere. The M2 was very popular with the Army Air Force, and many of the 8,510 built were used at airfields. In addition to being useful as a tug around the airfield, it also had a large air compressor mounted on the rear, which was very handy for airing up not only the tires of various vehicles, but also the landing gear of various aircraft. The towing draw-bar was especially designed to transfer as much weight as possible from the towed object to the tractor to increase the available traction effort.

G-150 M4 high speed tractor

The M4 18-ton high-speed tractor was designed to tow large field artillery pieces, haul ammunition for the same and transport the gun crew.

Allis-Chalmers developed and produced these vehicles in two load configurations. Vehicles produced to transport the Class A load had ammo bins for 90mm or 3 inch ammunition, while the Class B load was 155mm, 240mm or 8 inch ammo. The tractors had a built-in crane and hoist for handling the large ammunition.

Mounted on the rear of each vehicle was a PTO driven 30,000-pound capacity winch that was used when maneuvering and placing the artillery pieces. Production of the M4 began in March 1943 and continued through June 1945, during which time 5,552 vehicles had been completed.

High ground pressure and poor traction in certain terrain made it desirable to mount wider tracks on the tractors. Adding duckbill extensions on each end of the track shoe accomplished this; which in turn necessitated the spacing of the suspension units out from the hull. These vehicles, designated M4A1, were not introduced until June 1945, resulting in only 259 having been completed by August 1945.

Later, some of the 18-ton high-speed tractors were modified for increased ammunition stowage. These vehicles, which were identified by a C suffix on their model number, could transport only eight crewmen, versus the normal eleven.

The M4A2 series of vehicles was a result of a 1954 rebuild program carried out by Bowen-McLaughlin on the M4 tractors.

G-162 M5 high speed tractor

The M5 was a 13-ton high-speed, full-track, prime mover, which was utilized for the 90mm AA gun, 4.5" gun and 155mm howitzer. The M5 family of high-speed tractors was designed and built by International Harvester. They were built at International's Bettendorf, Iowa works and cost the government approximately $14,000.00 each. There were four variations of these vehicles.

The M5 was the base vehicle of the series, which had been prototyped as the T20. The tracks and suspension of the M5 high-speed tractor were based on those of the M3 light tank. The first T20 was shipped to the Aberdeen Proving Grounds on 4-30-42. After

Opposite page: Manufactured by International Harvester, the T21 Medium High-Speed Tractor featured a vertical volute suspension similar in appearance to that of the M3 Stuart Light Tank. The steel tracks were 14-inch block type. It could carry 24 rounds of 155mm ammunition. This example is fitted with the canopy top and curtains. **Top right:** A rear view of a T3E4 Light Tractor. **Middle right:** Front view of a T3E2 Light Tractor. **Bottom left:** The T5 Light Tractor was designed for use at airfields, moving aircraft and equipment. It was powered by a Ford V8 truck engine and weighed 2,690 pounds. **Bottom right:** One of two 40-gallon fuel tanks is prominently centered over the track on a T10 Medium Tractor. (All images courtesy of Patton Museum, Ft. Knox, KY)

successfully completing tests there, it was transferred to the Field Artillery Board at Ft. Bragg on 6-27-42. The first production model, serial number 503, was shipped on May 21, 1943. A total of 5,290 of these tractors was built during their 24-month production run, which began in May 1943.

Introduced in May 1945, the M5A1 was essentially a M5 with a steel cab fitted in lieu of the soft canvas cab structure of the M5. Comparatively few of these vehicles were built, with production totaling only 589, when the assembly line closed in August 1945.

A horizontal volute suspension system was developed for these tractors that was retrofitted after the war. When the vertical volute suspension of an M5 was replaced with the HVSS, the vehicle was redesignated M5A2. A similar change to a M5A1 resulted in a M5A3.

G-184 M6 high speed tractor

The vehicle that would evolve into the M6 high-speed tractor began as two vehicles, the T22 and T23 heavy tractors. The T22 had a fifth wheel coupling at the rear and was intended to tow the M1 240mm M1 Howitzer and the M1 8-inch gun when these weapons were equipped with semi-trailer transporters. The T23 had a cargo enclosure instead of the fifth wheel coupling of the T22, and it was

intended to tow the 4.7-inch T1 anti-aircraft gun.

When the Field Artillery Board decided to equip the M1 240mm M1 Howitzer and the M1 8-inch gun with the familiar full trailer carriage, there was no longer a need for the T22 and it was dropped. In June 1943, the T23 was standardized as the M6 38-ton high-speed tractor.

The M6 was the biggest of the big. Built by Allis-Chalmers, the M6 was larger than many WWII tanks. Its two huge Waukesha 145GZ straight-six gasoline engines gave it the muscle to tow up to 50,000 pounds. Torque converters coupled the two 817 cubic inch engines to a constant mesh two-speed transmission. Such literally ground-shaking power comes at a price, however, and the 250-gallon fuel tank only provided a range of 110 miles. Top speed with the weapon in tow was 20 miles per hour.

A 60,000-pound capacity drag winch mounted at the rear of the vehicle was used primarily when emplacing the field pieces it towed, but could also be used for vehicle recovery. The M6 also transported the gun crew on two rows of forward-facing seats in the cab. Depending upon the weapon being towed, from 20 to 24 rounds of artillery ammunition were carried in ammunition boxes at the rear of the tractor.

The dual engines occupied the middle portion of the vehicle, with their radiators on either side. An M49C ring mount for the M2 Browning .50 caliber machine gun was mounted on the roof for defense.

Various delays prevented production of these huge machines from beginning until February 1944, with the result that only 1,235 had been built by August 1945.

G-252 M8A1 cargo tractor

In 1945, the Stillwell Board (War Department Equipment Board) re-addressed the matter of high-speed tractors. These documents today provide some insight into the development of what was to become the M8A1. The Board stated that requirements existed for 13-ton, 18-ton and 38-ton tractors, all capable of transporting a payload, as well as acting as a prime mover. It was suggested that these tractors have performance such that they could operate in convoy with wheeled vehicles, yet have a parts and off-road performance commonality with fully tracked combat vehicles.

Recommendations from the field were included in appendices to the Stillwell Board Report. The Mediterranean Theater recommended no further development of high-speed tractors, that emphasis instead be placed on wheeled prime movers. The U.S. Army Forces, Pacific (AFPAC) agreed that there should be no further development of high-speed tractors. AFPAC further stated that in the event there was more work on high speed tractors, that consideration should be given to lowering ground pressure, including power transmission to both tracks during turns and on providing optional blades for tractors assigned to artillery batteries.

Top left: The T2 Heavy Tractor, a General Motors prototype, had the track and suspension from an M2A1 Medium Tank and light armor up to a half-inch thick. Top right: An Allis-Chalmers M1 Medium Tractor is towing a 105mm howitzer and trailer. Bottom left: An International Harvester M1 Heavy Tractor in use as an artillery prime mover for the prototype "Long Tom" rifle. Bottom right: Based on the M10 Gun Motor Carriage chassis, the M35 Tractor (fitted here with a non-standard cover) was an expedient pending the deployment of the M6 high-speed tractor. Note the Jeep windshield in use on the non-standard cover. The M35 was typically not issued with a cover, but GI's always seemed to find a way! (All images courtesy of Patton Museum, Ft. Knox, KY)

The M8A1 was originally known as the M8E2 (the basic M8 existed as a concept only). As recommended by the Stillwell Board, this high-speed tractor shared its AOS-895-3 engine and transmission with the M41 light tank. Also as recommended, the M8 series tractors all had a provision for the installation of the T8E4 hydraulic bulldozer kit.

In July 1950, Allis-Chalmers was given an order for 480 of these tractors, all of which were completed by the end of 1955. When the engine was upgraded to the fuel injected AOS-895-5, the vehicle's classification was changed to M8A2. These vehicles were designed to tow artillery loads in the 18,000 to 32,000 pound range and to carry cargo weighing up to 7.5 tons. The fuel-injected, six-cylinder engine provided a top speed of 40 mph.

To control the Allison CD-500-3 cross-drive transmission the driver used handlebar-type steering. The tractor could cross a seven-foot ditch, climb a 2.5 foot vertical wall and ford up to 3.5 feet without preparation.

The M8A1 and A2 were the last high-speed tractors procured in series by the U.S. Army. The age of towed artillery it seemed, had passed, to be supplanted by self-propelled artillery.

A pallet of parts boxes marked "The Cleveland Tractor Co." is strapped to the front bumper of a new M2 High-Speed Tractor, commonly known as the Cletrac. The tracks were continuous rubber bands with steel cables fused to forged steel cross members molded in. (U.S. Army)

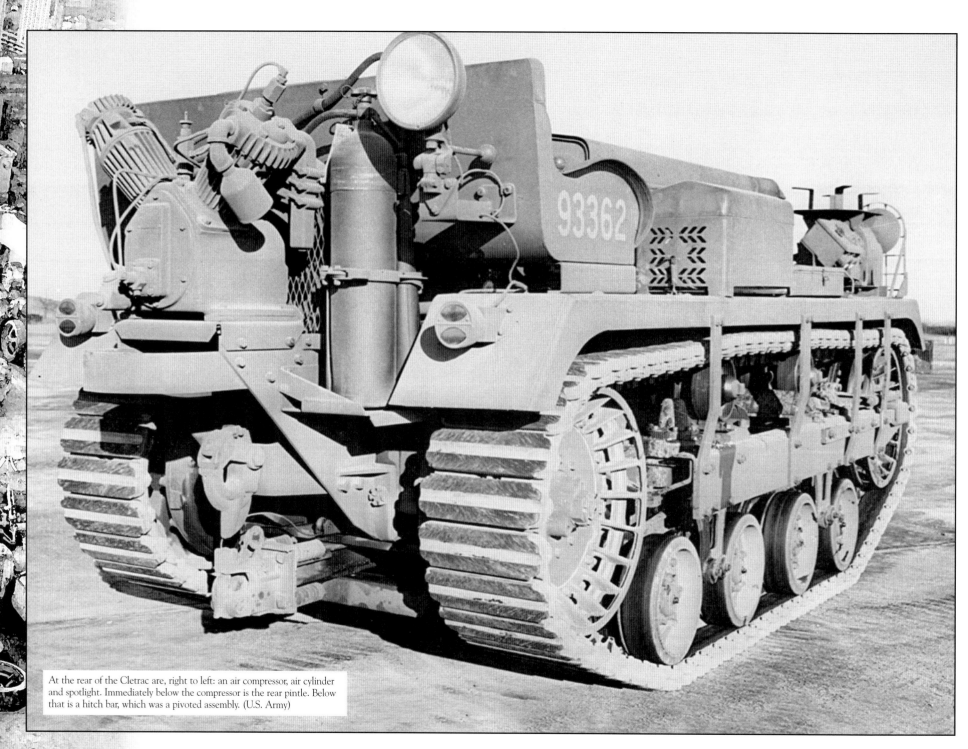

At the rear of the Cletrac are, right to left: an air compressor, air cylinder and spotlight. Immediately below the compressor is the rear pintle. Below that is a hitch bar, which was a pivoted assembly. (U.S. Army)

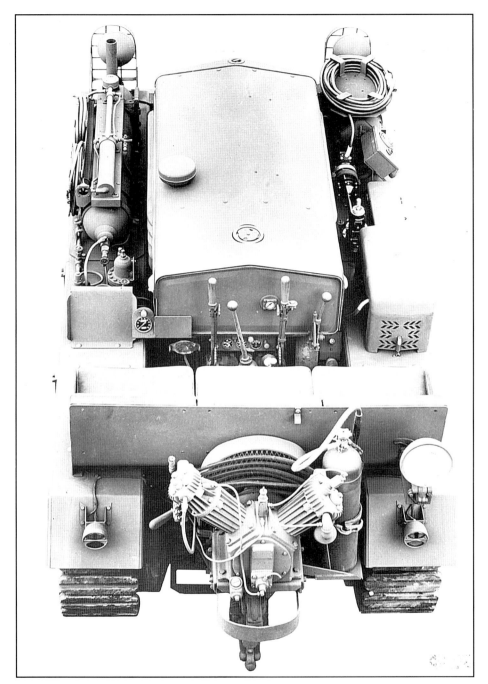

Left: The driver of the M2 sat in the center seat. The box with vents toward the rear of the right fender was the battery cover. **Right:** This M2 lacks the radiator guard but has the protective cover for the belt drive from the front power takeoff to the General Electric power generator on the right front fender. Notice "Cletrac" stamped on the radiator cover. Below the belt drive is the 7,500-pound-capacity reversible, single-drive winch. (U.S. Army)

Using a pry bar, a workman eases the right-hand track over the idler wheel. The M2 is on a truck, so its bogie wheels are raised above the floor. The M2 operator's manual directed that tracks were to be adjusted so that there was no visible sag anywhere along the top run of the track. Also visible are the steering and shift levers to the left of the engine hood and the windshield support assembly above the hood. (Deere & Company Archives)

The fenders on each side of the Cletrac were two-part assemblies, with front and rear assemblies. In this photograph, the front right fender is being lowered into place. Just visible above the bumper is the empty winch drum. The long horizontal tube below the bumper is the winch cable roller. Bolted to the steel front bumper channel were two wooden blocks. (Deere & Company Archives)

These two Cletracs on the factory floor have had their compressor guards installed. Extending from the tops of the vertical members of the guards are carriers, around which towropes were wrapped. The tractor on the left has its battery hood in place, while the storage battery on the one to right is exposed. The factory-specified battery was the Willard WH-25-6. (Deere & Company Archives)

Arrayed on the right fender of an M2 HST are, left to right, the battery hood; toolbox; generator switch box with four outlets; General Electric 1,000-watt, 110-volt DC power generator; and headlight and guard. The large horizontal frame above the bogie wheels was called the guide bar. The vertical braces between the guide bar and the fender were called irons. The windshield assembly has been installed, with its single, center-mounted electric windshield wiper. (U.S. Army)

Prominent in this rear view of an M2 are the heavy-duty pintle and, below it, hitch bar assembly on a swivel mount. The air compressor guard on this vehicle lacks the towrope carriers. Notice the bracket assembly that the rear spotlight is mounted to and the blackout tail light below it. (U.S. Army)

The bracket to the right of the right rear taillight is the rear push pole carrier. Found on all M2s from serial numbers 7JA000 and IDA000 up, the brackets were mounted on the front and rear of the right fender. The carrier swiveled out when the pole was stored on it and was swung in and secured with the strap clamp when not in use, as seen here. Either a push pole or tow pole, used in moving aircraft around, could be secured in the carrier by the strap clamp. (U.S. Army)

Viewed from above, the top of the transmission is visible in front of the center (driver's) seat. To either side of it are the steering levers. Also visible here are the fuel filler cap just behind the edge of the windshield and the single wiper motor. A high-pressure air tank is on the front left fender. Coiled above it are two high-pressure hoses. (U.S. Army)

The complete cab cover has been installed on this Cletrac. Supported by a tubular bow assembly, it comprised a top/rear section and side curtains. The top and curtains attached to the windshield with snaps; elsewhere, web straps were used to secure the canvas. For heating the cab in cold weather, a hot-air heater was attached to the engine manifold. (U.S. Army)

Straps attached to Footman loops on the seat back and fenders held down the cab cover. Immediately below the bottom of the rear panel of the cab cover is a narrow rack. When not in use, the cover was folded and stored on this rack. The grilles on the side of the hood were characteristic of later Cletracs. Earlier versions of the tractor had long louvers on the sides of the hood for ventilation. (U.S. Army)

An early-model Cletrac is being used as a prime mover for an M1918 155mm howitzer. The deep sand and the 9,000-pound load of the M1918 are causing the rear of the tractor dig deep into the sand. The long louvers on the side of the hood are clearly visible here. Despite the straining of the M2, the 155mm howitzer does not appear to be budging. This may be a pre-production MG1, predecessor to the M2. (NARA)

Two M2s are seen here on a transport trailer. The front vehicle has a cab cover with the rear plastic vision panels broken out. Directly in front of the sergeant's face is a knob for clamping the hinged windshield. Either steel ice grousers or, in this case, individual rubber track blocks were bolted to the continuous tracks. Bolt heads for fastening the blocks are visible on the underside of the upper track. These rubber track blocks lack the center cutouts seen on the tracks of some M2s. Notice the fire extinguisher on the side of the seat and the broken-out stop light lens. (NARA)

It was exactly this sort of muddy environment that made Cletrac so popular—and effective—at the airfields of England and northwestern Europe. The tractor could move aircraft and equipment around in some of the worst imaginable conditions. A ground crewman in winter flight suit adjusts a high-pressure air hose. The wedge-shaped object on the fender to his right is the passenger's footrest. The number 97780 is stenciled on the side of the seat, while a temporary number, 6252AA, has been whitewashed on the seatback. (NARA)

In the absence of an air compressor guard with towrope keepers, a long towrope has been draped from the seat to the pintle. As this photograph attests, Cletracs at army airfields could get every bit as weathered as armored vehicles in the field. (John Adams-Graf Collection)

Proving its utility, this M2 is used by a ground crew to refuel a Curtiss P-40 on Nanumea Island in the Ellice Islands, December 1943. Its load is a Heil 2W Type F-2 Fuel-Servicing Semitrailer. This 2,000-gallon trailer was unique in that it had twin gas driven pumps in the rear with a capacity of 160 gallons per minute. (NASM)

Seen in a motor vehicle repair depot at the airbase in Moulins, France, in the spring of 1948, these two M2 tractors are sporting their new Air Force serial numbers. They both also appear to be newly painted yellow for maximum visibility on the flightline. Accordingly to the original caption, the Master Sergeant seen in the middle distance is the sole non-commissioned-officer-in-charge of the more than 250 vehicles on the lot for repairs—a fascinating assortment of WW2 2.5-ton trucks and bomb service vehicles. (NASM)

The cover bow assembly and the top of the cab cover are installed on this preserved Cletrac. Many of the accessories have been removed, allowing a clear view of the mount for the air compressor. The primary purpose of the Cletrac's air compressor was to inflate shock absorber struts on aircraft. It had two outlet hoses: one delivering pressures up to 1,000 psi, and another for pressures up to 1,500 psi. The small canister attached to the right cylinder of the compressor is the air intake filter.

A well maintained Cletrac of the Air Force Museum at Wright-Patterson Air Force Base still sports its left-fender air tank and hoses, to the aft of which are the associated valves and pressure regulators. The vertical tube in front of the air tank is variously described in Cletrac manuals as a flagpole holder and a crane holder. (Mike Kalbfleisch)

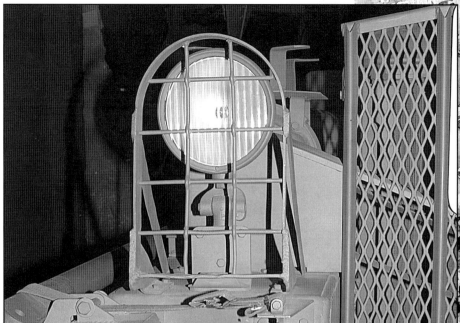

Top left: Visible behind the grille of the radiator guard is the drive belt for the power generator. Behind the cutout in the grille is the power takeoff shift lever. **Top right:** The headlights, actually referred to as spotlights in the Cletrac manuals, are mounted on swiveling bases. The front push pole bracket is just visible at the left bottom of the photograph. **Bottom left:** The adjusting screw mechanism for the idler wheel is visible alongside and to the rear of the wheel. Notice the bolts and nuts around the inner edge of the track assembly, by which the rubber track blocks are fastened to the track. Each track block has three bolts embedded in it—one near the center and one near each end. **Bottom right:** On this Cletrac, the air hose reels are positioned vertically. On some other Cletracs, the reels were in a tilted position. The object on top of the hood is the air cleaner. (Mike Kalbfleisch)

M4 High Speed Tractor

The 18-ton M4 high speed tractor was designed mainly as a prime mover for the 90mm anti-aircraft gun, 3-inch gun, 155mm gun, and 8-inch and 240mm howitzers. The large engine grille is a prominent feature of this tractor. Above the grille is the air pre-cleaner. The side curtains overlap when open. On the roof over the rear passenger compartment is a stowage box. Notice the font emplacing pintle under the front bumper. Note the heavy wire guards over the front headlights. (U.S. Army)

Above the engine grille on the right side of the M4 is the muffler hood. The ammunition box identifies this vehicle as the Class B type, used for carrying 155mm, 240mm, or 8-inch ammunition. This type was fitted with a rear swing-down tailgate and a swivel crane to assist in loading and unloading the heavy rounds. The crane is just visible above the top rear of the ammunition box. Also visible here are the rear floodlight wire guards and the hold chains for the rear door. (U.S. Army)

The inside of the M4's ammunition box was painted white. There was no metal hood for the box, only a removable canvas cover. The swivel crane is to the left of the box. Over the cab is a Browning .50-caliber M2 machine gun on an M49C ring mount, in front of which is stowed a machine gun tripod. Spare track links are stored in front of the tripod. (U.S. Army)

This M4 is the Class A type used for moving 3-inch guns or 90mm antiaircraft guns. A characteristic of this type is the ammunition box with side doors. The rectangles on either side of the star on the front of the tractor are cab ventilators. They had internal hinges and could be opened from the inside of the vehicle when necessary. When closed, the side curtains were secured with web straps through Footman loops. Interestingly, this tractor is missing its front emplacement pintle. (U.S. Army)

The side doors of the 90mm ammunition boxes were secured shut with large latches on each side. The PTO-driven winch drum with its full reel of cable is faintly visible through the oblong opening below the rear ammunition box door. Below that opening is the rear pintle, which consists of a universal swivel and yoke, unlike the fixed pintle of the M4 designed to tow the 155mm gun and 240mm howitzer. The devices with chains to either side of the pintle are the service and emergency air brake couplings for trailers. Outboard of these are access panels for the winch. (U.S. Army)

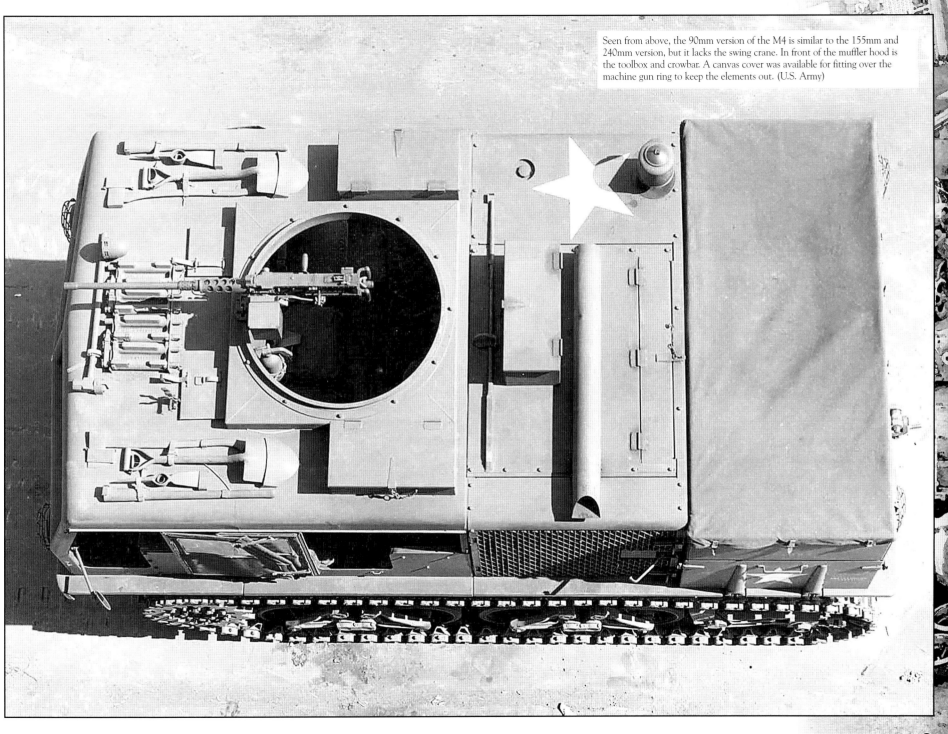

Seen from above, the 90mm version of the M4 is similar to the 155mm and 240mm version, but it lacks the swing crane. In front of the muffler hood is the toolbox and crowbar. A canvas cover was available for fitting over the machine gun ring to keep the elements out. (U.S. Army)

The M4A1 high-speed tractor was essentially the M4 with the suspension wheels and sprockets extended out from the hull, to enable the addition of duckbill extensions to the tracks. This example has the duckbill extensions on the inside and outside of the tracks, but sometimes they were placed only on the outside. To accommodate the wider tracks, a wider fender and front bumper were added to the M4A1. (U.S. Army)

The Class B ammunition box of this M4A1 has louvered side vents. The suspension and track extensions added fourteen inches to the width of the vehicle. Notice the base of the crane stanchion protruding through the bottom of the rear overhang of the ammunition box, to the left of the tailgate. The fuel filler line and cap extends out from the right-hand opening on the rear plate below the ammunition box. (U.S. Army)

A full load of 12 rounds of 240mm howitzer ammunition is stored in the ammunition box of this M4A1. The crane is not in place, but the chain hoist is lying on a hold-down plate for the projectiles. The powder charges are in the canisters outboard of the projectiles. The widened fender of the M4A1 is apparent in this view. (U.S. Army)

An M4 tows a 155mm Long Tom, with a crewman manning the ring-mounted .50-caliber machine gun. The blackout headlight and blackout marker light are in the quarter-round recess on the cowl. In addition to the two cab vents on the cowl of the M4, there were three vents with grilles and thin metal doors on the front of the hull. This tractor also lacks the front positioning pintle usually welded to the front of the M4. This pintle was used for moving around artillery pieces once detached from the rear pintle. The thin metal doors for the three hull vents are open.

Twin M4's each with a Class B ammunition boxes await transport overseas at the port of Hampton Roads, in late 1943. These vehicles are in the very first stages of preparation for their ocean voyage, as they lack even the covers for the tops of the ammunition bins. Like most M4's, these two tractors mount the cleated T49 metal tracks for maximum traction on soft ground. One of the goals of high-speed tractor design was commonality of parts and the M4 shared the drive sprocket, and therefore the tracks, of the M4 series of medium tanks. (Library of Virginia)

At the PAC Combat training center on Oahu, Hawaii various field modifications were tested and the subsequent advice was then sent on to the combat zone. Here, "Amos," an M4 with a ventilated Class B box, presses through the waist high elephant grass (inset) on April 15th, 1945. Twelve inch wooden extensions have been fitted to each of the T49 track blocks in an effort to lower the ground pressure of the tractor. (NARA)

Members of the Utah National Guard prepare to emplace their 155mm gun during an exercise in June 1950. The scenery is courtesy of Ft. Douglas, Utah. In contrast to the previous photos, this tractor mounts the T51 rubber block track. These became common in National Guard and other garrison units, since they were more kind to road surfaces. Like many peacetime vehicles, this one lacks its typically mounted .50 caliber machine gun. (NARA)

An M4 of an unidentified anti-aircraft unit hauls ass though the South Korean town of Taegu during the early stages of the conflict. The windshields and cab vents (either side of the star) are open. The lubrication placard on the .50-caliber ammunition box appears to be white with black letters. Since the men on top of the tractor are armed with M1 carbines, is it safe to say they are the gun crew, not infantrymen hitching a ride. The crew has opened the front windshields for better ventilation in the hot Korean summer. (NARA)

Seen here in the Korean town of Waegen in August of 1950, is a little photographed companion of the M4, the M23 ammunition trailer. The Utility Trailer Mfg. Co. in Los Angeles manufactured over 1,700 of these 8-ton trailers between 1944 and 1945. When towed by the M4 or M6 high-speed tractors, the M23 was to be used in conjunction with the M5 limber, which was also used with the 155mm gun and 8-inch howitzer. Without the M5, the 7.5-ton Mack NO typically towed it. Its load was either 32 complete rounds of 240mm ammunition, 60 8-inch rounds, or 96 155mm gun rounds. (NARA)

A Class B M4 mounting T48 rubber chevron tracks of the 1st Cavalry Division rests outside the town of Taegu on September 15, 1951. The national star on the cowl exhibits noticeable overspray on the right and bottom. Inside the cab, above the soldier's left hand, is a box for stowing .50-caliber ammunition. The large placard on the front of the box contains lubrication instructions for the tractor. The small holes on the edge of the fender are for attaching a side skirt, seldom used in the field. (NARA)

A wooden bin has been constructed on top of the 90mm ammunition box of this M4 of the 40th Antiaircraft Artillery Brigade, Seventh Army, in Germany in 1956. A spare tire for a 90mm antiaircraft gun is mounted on the rear. Both of the trailer air brake couplings above the pintle have been painted a light color, evidently white. The ammunition box of the M4 to the left has been removed, exposing the rear of the engine compartment. Both tractors mount the T48 rubber block tracks, a good compromise of traction and road friendly. (NARA)

California National Guard crewmen of a 90mm antiaircraft gun dismount from an M4 during coastal maneuvers in 1949. Curiously, the ammunition box is the Class B box designed for 155mm and larger rounds, not the Class A box designed to hold 90mm ammunition (perhaps none is carried?). The side skirts are rarely seen in photos of this tractor. Notice the step cutout near the front of the skirt. This tractor carries sparse markings; only the agency identification and registration number are visible. (NARA)

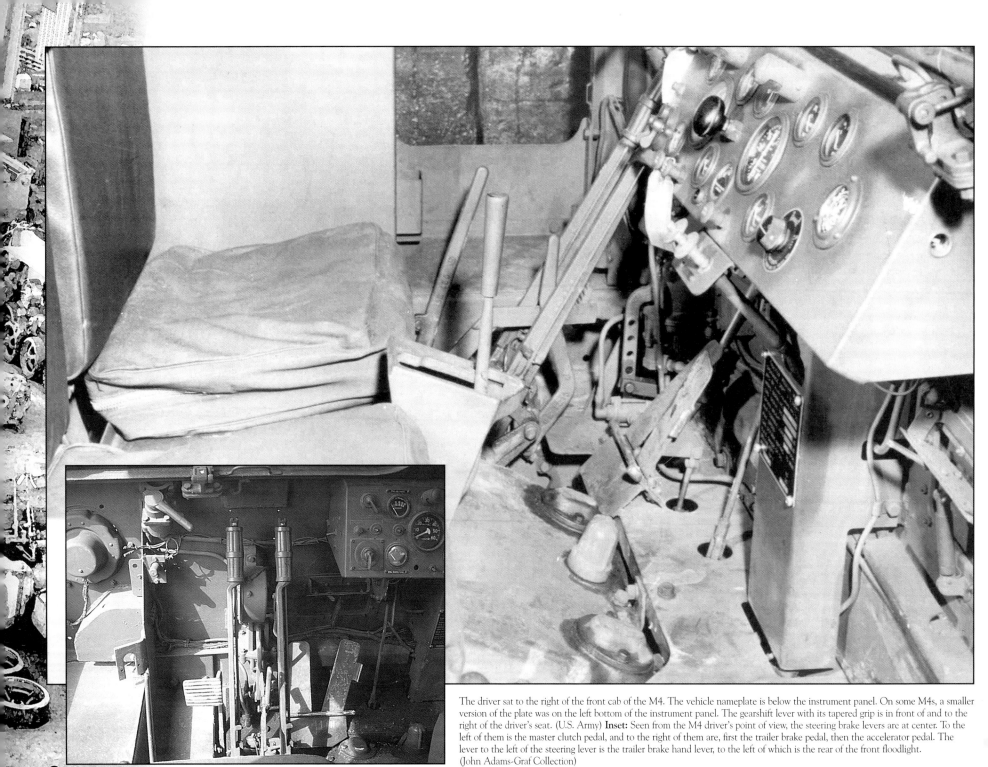

The driver sat to the right of the front cab of the M4. The vehicle nameplate is below the instrument panel. On some M4s, a smaller version of the plate was on the left bottom of the instrument panel. The gearshift lever with its tapered grip is in front of and to the right of the driver's seat. (U.S. Army) **Inset:** Seen from the M4 driver's point of view, the steering brake levers are at center. To the left of them is the master clutch pedal, and to the right of them are, first the trailer brake pedal, then the accelerator pedal. The lever to the left of the steering lever is the trailer brake hand lever, to the left of which is the rear of the front floodlight. (John Adams-Graf Collection)

The large placard on the side of the .50-caliber ammunition box at the far end of the cab contains general operating instructions. This photo gives a good view of the latches and swing-arms of the windshields. The fire extinguisher, secured by a bracket clamp, is at the right. Notice that the rear-view mirror has been pulled inside the curtain. (U.S. Army) **Inset:** Another view of the driver's controls and instrument panel of a restored M4. (John Adams-Graf Collection)

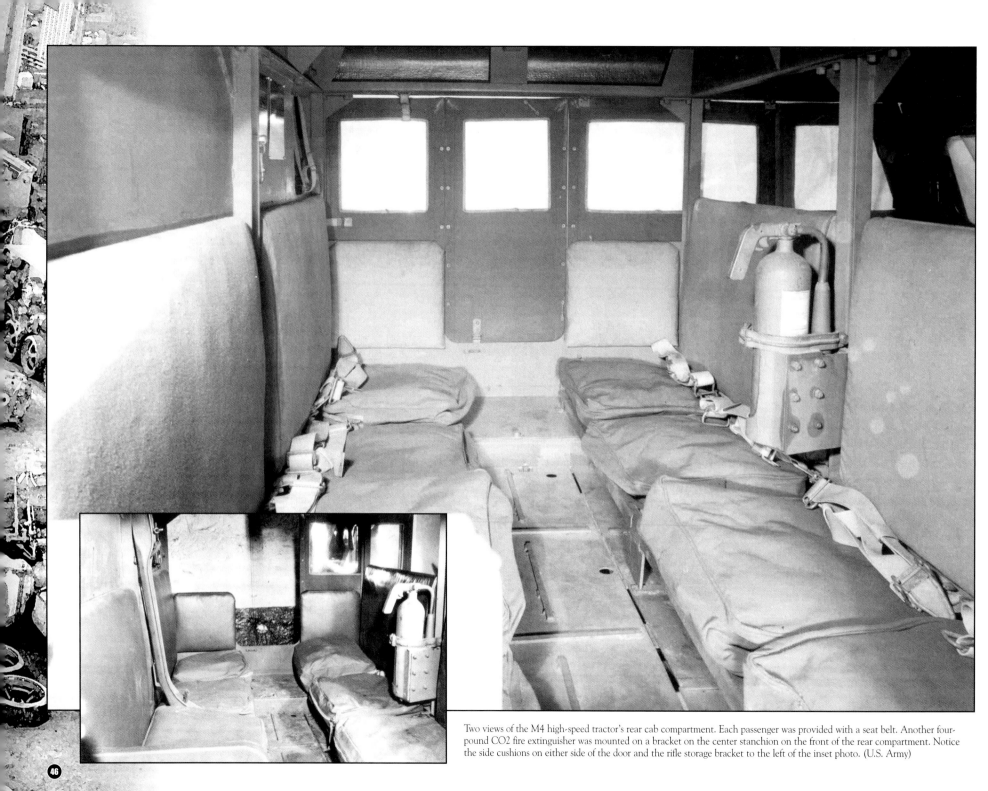

Two views of the M4 high-speed tractor's rear cab compartment. Each passenger was provided with a seat belt. Another four-pound CO2 fire extinguisher was mounted on a bracket on the center stanchion on the front of the rear compartment. Notice the side cushions on either side of the door and the rifle storage bracket to the left of the inset photo. (U.S. Army)

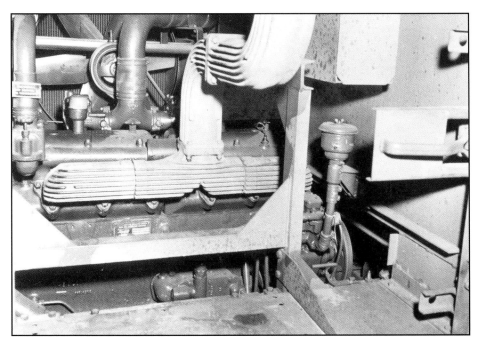

Top left: This is the M4's engine compartment, as seen through the opened engine grille on the right side of the tractor. The prominent features are the finned exhaust manifold and, extending above it, the upper and lower elbows of the exhaust. The fan is visible on the far side of the compartment. **Top right:** The opened rear door of a Class A ammunition box reveals several water cans. The chain holds a fastener for latching the door shut. **Bottom left:** The tailgate of a Class B M4 ammunition box has been lowered, revealing the interior of the compartment and the chain hoist suspended from the swivel crane. The taillights with their protectors flank the opening. Curiously, the inside of the tailgate is painted white; usually in U.S. Army practice, the insides of doors were painted the same color as the exterior of the vehicle. **Bottom right:** The lowered right-side door of the ammunition box exposes the interior and the shell racks for 90mm rounds. There was a similar compartment and racks on the opposite side of the tractor. (U.S. Army)

The power winch cable is hooked over a towing clevis. The louvered cover visible though the opening above the clevis is for the automatic brake of the power winch. The two tail floodlights were used for illumination when handling towed weapons and equipment in the dark. The pintle lacks the universal yoke usually found on 90mm M4s. The restored vehicle seen here and on the next page, sports road friendly T51 rubber block tracks. (John Adams-Graf Collection)

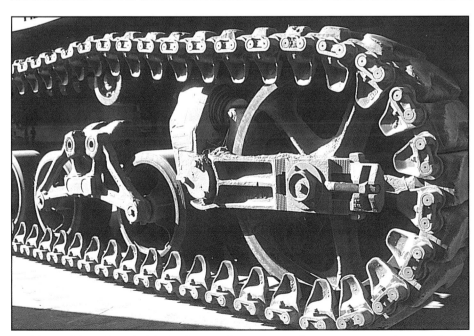

Top left: Seen left to right on the left side of an M4 with ammunition and engine compartment doors open are: the 90mm shell rack, air cleaner (with cyclone-type air pre-cleaner on top, above the compartment) and radiator. It was necessary to service the air cleaner daily by removing the dust from it. **Top right:** The large latch is for securing the ammunition door. The small handles above and below it are for latching the engine grille. **Bottom left:** The features of the idler wheel are well portrayed here. The yoke (also called the idler arm), the horizontal arm that bore the wheel, pivoted on the idler support bracket in front of the wheel. A volute spring provided shock absorption. **Bottom right:** From right to left on this M4 are the left sprocket, T51 tracks, towing hook, vent cover and positioning pintle. (Top left, U.S. Army, all others John Adams-Graf Collection)

Left: A view of the driver's controls and instrument panel of an M4A1. The two light-colored knobs at the bottom of the instrument panel are (left) engine stop control and (right) choke control. The large black knob protruding from the center of the instrument panel is the primer pump, while the black knob to the right of the photo is the electric brake load control. **Top right:** The rear compartment of this M4A1, as viewed through the right side, is cluttered with gear and shows the effects of hard use. **Bottom right:** This shot of the interior of an M4A1 engine compartment was taken from the right side of the vehicle. The angle-iron structure is the radiator-supporting frame. The torque-converter oil radiator assembly, air cleaner, and associated hoses and lines were attached to the supporting frame. When the frame was unbolted from the engine compartment, those bulky components could easily be hoisted out of the compartment for repair or replacement. (U.S. Army)

M5 High Speed Tractor

The M5 13-ton high-speed tractor was designed as a prime mover for artillery pieces ranging in size from the M2 105mm howitzer up to the M1 4.5-inch gun. On this example, the windshield is folded down and secured by latches to the small cowl. On each side of the cowl is a bi-folding door. Below the cowl is the power winch, which had a maximum pull capacity of 15,000 pounds. (U.S. Army)

The M5 had a six-blade, 28-inch-diameter fan at the rear of the vehicle. A heavy-duty grille protected it, at the top right of which was a deflector for the engine exhaust (not always seen on M5s). Flanking the grille on either side were screen doors leading to a narrow passageway that provided access to the radiators and other components on either side of the engine compartment. The pintle hook swiveled and was spring loaded, to absorb the shock of sudden lurches when pulling a load. The nomenclature for the box-shaped mount was the pintle hook housing. (U.S. Army)

On the top of the rear compartment of this M5 are two sets of pioneer tools on the cover of the powder boxes, two top radiator doors covered with fine screen and the engine compartment hood. The larger door at the rear of the hood provided access to the engine, while the smaller front door gave access to the air cleaner and battery. In the center compartment are four seats for crewmembers and the shell box. In the forward compartment, the driver sits at the center, flanked by seats for four more crewmen. (U.S. Army)

This M5 is wearing its canopy top and curtains, fitted over a bow of slip-fit pipes and brackets. The joints of the bow parts were color coded for ease of assembly. The clear panels over the front doors could be opened along with the doors. The tracks are the cleated T36E6, which are parts shaded (along with the drive sprockets) from the M3/M5 series of light tanks. Notice the siren near the bottom of the cowl. (U.S. Army)

The M5 canopy and curtains are seen from the rear in this photo. The boxes on both sides of the rear of the vehicle held powder charges and were removable. Each box mounted a fixed floodlight, a blackout light, and two red reflectors. The two doors on either side of the pinion (including the one with 27 stenciled on it) were for small compartments, each of which held a welded steel gun chest. Interestingly, this vehicle mounts the steel chevron block track. (U.S. Army)

Bonjour, a mud-spattered M5 of the 773rd FA Bn. waits its turn to cross a Treadway bridge over the Moselle river on November 11th, 1994. A good deal of graffiti has been painted on the vehicle, including signs for "Men" and "Women" next to the front doors. Notice the two data plates below the Bonjour. The tractor appears to be carrying more than the usual complement of nine men. The crew has elected to erect the canopy, but not the curtains. Two more M5s with canopies are following the two Jeeps. (NARA)

Troops unload large-caliber projectiles from tandem M10 ammunition trailers towed by an M5 on Biak Island in the pacific on June 8th 1944. The various packing materials for the 155mm howitzer are of interest. The hole at the bottom of the tailgate of the M10 trailer was to enable it to clear a pintle on the rear bumper. (NARA)

This M5 carries an interesting array of gear, including knapsacks, tents or bedrolls and large shocks of hay, possibly for later use for camouflage purposes. Although the canopy is not in place, the clear curtain panels are still attached to the tops of the front doors, which have been secured in the open position. The M5 is towing a 155mm howitzer. It appears to be giving assistance to an armored Caterpillar D7 with La Plant-Coate R71 angle blade. (NARA)

An M5 of the 196th FA treks along a dusty Korean trace, pulling a 155mm howitzer in April of 1951. The windshield is folded down and protected by its canvas cover. The two front doors are open and secured in their folded position. The tracks are T16 type, with smooth rubber blocks. There appears to be a permanent steel frame over the rear passenger/ammo compartment that may have been the field modification MWO ORD G 162-W3 that allowed a .50-cal. machine gun to be added to the M5. There is also a lightweight pipe bow in front, holding a metal canopy frame and canvas top. (NARA)

The crews of three M5 high-speed tractors of the 82nd FA (155mm) take a break along a creek in Korea with a fourth M5 partially visible at the far left. The 82nd was part of the 1st Cavalry Division and was traveling to support the expanding Pusan perimeter at the time this photo was taken in September 1950. The crew of the forward vehicles appears less than happy to have their picture taken. A substantial amount of gear has been stowed atop the vehicles, including the forward canopies. (NARA)

Left: Details of the cowl and the right bi-folding door leading to the front cab are evident in this view. A section of steel-wire mesh welded to the bumper provides a non-slip tread, facilitating crew entry and egress to the cab. The vertical latch on the front of the cowl could be swung up and attached to the lowered windshield with the wing nut visible on the corner of the windshield, seen here with its canvas cover. Below the cowl is the winch, with the gear case emphasized in this photo. **Right.** A view through the partially opened bi-folding front door, with the bottom of the ring mount visible at the top.

Top left: Early M5s lacked a front positioning pinion; this example on a saddle mount on the bumper appears to have been a later modification. The Gar Wood winch was driven by a shaft from the transmission and had a capacity of 15,000 pounds. **Top right:** The drum bearing and drag brake of the winch are evident in this view. The horizontal line connecting to the winch is the air pipe. The M5's winch was equipped with both a drag brake and, on the other side, an automatic brake. **Bottom left:** The M5's headlight and attached blackout marker light were on

a swivel mount (bottom). When the latch above the top of the brush guard was pulled up, the headlight assembly could be swung out and down, allowing access to the lamp and electrical connections. To the right of the headlight is an amber reflector. **Bottom right:** Above the pintle housing are the trailer service air brake coupler (left) and trailer emergency air brake coupler (right). The circular fixture to the right of the pintle is the trailer electrical coupling socket.

Top left: Looking aft from the rear crew compartment is the engine hood. The grilles on either side of it provided ventilation for the two radiators, which were situated fore and aft on each side of the engine compartment. The grilles were hinged to the powder boxes and could be opened to allow access to the radiators and radiator shutters. **Top right:** In the engine compartment of an M5, viewed from the rear, the air cleaner is partially visible at top left. The radiators are on either side of the compartment. The two oil filters are to the right of the Continental R6572 six-cylinder engine. **Bottom left:** The top and ring mount of the MWO ORD G 162-W3 field modification. A cradle assembly and carriage are mounted on the M49C ring mount of an M5. Below are the two right-hand crew seats in the rear of the cab. The seat cushions were secured in place with snaps. **Bottom right:** The thick, horizontal beam is the suspension frame. It was attached to the hull by cross members and its function was to support the bogies, trailing idler wheels, and track support idlers (or return rollers).

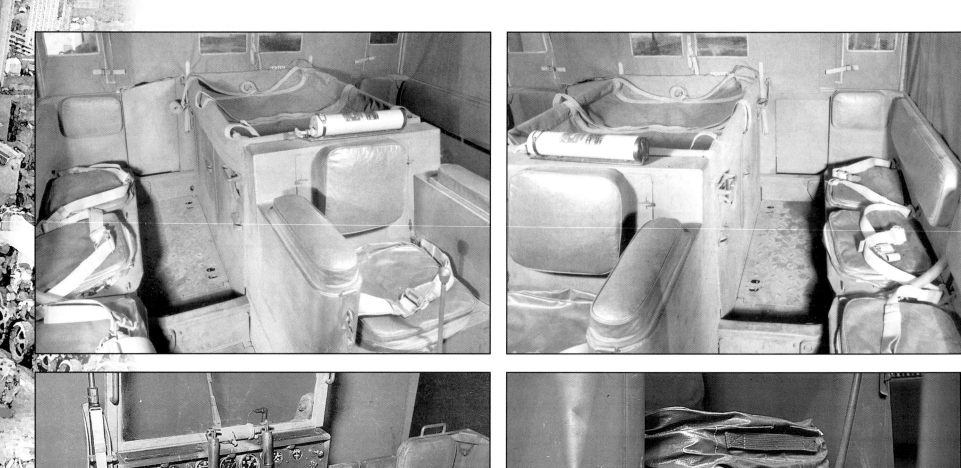

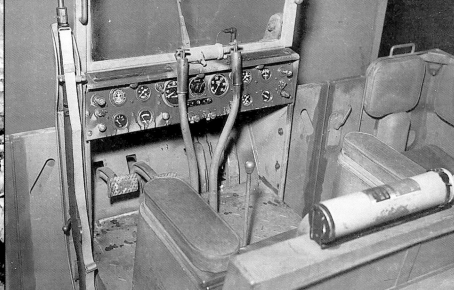

Top left: Viewed from the front of an M5 cab with top and curtains installed, the driver's seat is to the right. Four crew seats were on either side of the compartment, facing inward. Each of the driver's arm rests folded up to allow access to toolboxes. A canvas cover is over the shell box, as is a small fire extinguisher. **Top right:** A view of the right side of the cab. Two platform doors were on the floor of each side of the cab; they covered storage compartments. **Bottom left:** Looking over the M5 driver's seat, to the left is an M1903 Springfield rifle stored in a universal rifle bracket. The service clutch pedal is to the right of the rifle; next to that pedal but hidden by the armrest is the emergency clutch pedal. The lever in front of the seat is the transmission gearshift. **Bottom right:** This photo shows the bottom of the arm rests/tool boxes flanking the driver's seat, the driver's seat cushion, floor plate and gearshift. The controls on the front of the seat platform are, from left to right: winch hand lever, starter control hand lever, fuel tank selector valve knob, choke hand lever, and fan clutch hand lever.

M5A1 High Speed Tractor

The M5A1 shared the same vertical volute suspension, engine, clutch, and power train as the M5, but varied considerably from the M5 in other aspects. A major difference was in the design of the cab. The M5A1's cab had a permanent metal canopy frame, with a ring mount for a .50-caliber machine gun. Crew entry and egress was through two metal doors on each side of the cab. The tractor also had a large cowl with two windshields, and two shell boxes accessible from the sides of the vehicle. (U.S. Army)

The rear of the M5A1 was identical to that of the M5. Notice the travel lock for the machine gun on the rear of the cab top. The rear reflectors were red, while the forward reflectors were amber. The muffler was mounted transversely under the top of the fan guard. The round object near the top of the guard was an exhaust deflector. (U.S. Army)

As opposed to the M5 with its seating for nine men, the M5A1 could seat 11, with the driver's seat to the left of center. The shell boxes are on either side of the rear of the crew compartment; the perforated plates in the boxes are shell retainers, which are held down with clamps to secure the tops of the shells. At the rear of the engine hood is the cap for the cooling system filler bowl. (U.S. Army)

The canvas top and curtains have been installed on this M5A1, including covers for the shell boxes. When not in use, the curtains were stored in compartments behind two of the crew seats. Unlike the M5, only the drum of the M5A1's power winch was exposed. To either side of the drum are access doors for the winch mechanism. The headlights are of the same hinged design as those of the M5. The small perforations at the top of the column between the windshields are for the electric horn. The brackets between the fenders and the bumper are mounting steps. (U.S. Army)

U.S.A.
9142907 S

251

The front M5A1 of a field artillery observation battalion is towing a trailer containing the SCR-584 counter battery radar. This was a derivative of the WW2 SCR-584 AAA radar, but installed on a much smaller platfrom. The unit was mounted on a slightly modified M13 trailer and was used exclusively for counter battery fire. As indicated by the other photos in the sequence, the markings on the front of forward tractor are "2626-B." This was not a known unit and it could be a deliberate attempt at subterfuge, as the radars where considered top secret at this time. Field artillery observation battalions deployed in Korea were the 1st, 2nd, 61st, 92nd and the 235th. While the front tractor has three national stars on the cowl, the other has only two small stars. (NARA)

An M5A1 with side curtains installed negotiates a muddy slough in April of 1951, while towing a 155mm howitzer. This tractor belongs to the 196th FA Bn., which was part of the 8th Army at the time. Interestingly, the tractor is carefully avoiding the freshly planted rice paddy in the foreground just outside of the Korean town of Taki Gol. Immediately behind the M5A1 is an M5. This M5 appears to be one with a metal canopy installed over the rear of the cab. There are at least three tires sticking up above the rear of tractor. (NARA)

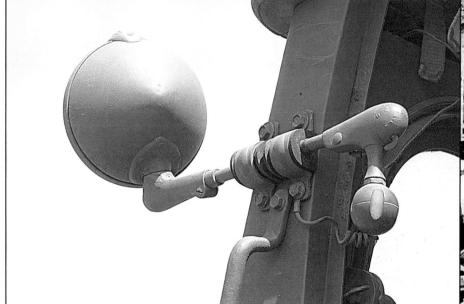

Top left: A view from the front left of an M5A1 includes the headlight mount and front reflectors. The two cab vents are ajar. The bolted-on panel under the national star is the hand hole cover, providing access to electrical connections when performing maintenance or removing the cowl. **Top right:** Mounted on the front bumper of M5A1s are two towing hooks and, between them, the front positioning pintle. The towing hook of the winch cable has been secured to the pintle. **Bottom left:** A siren has been mounted on the side of the winch compartment at the front of this M5A1. The April 1950 tech manual for M5A1 shows only a horn on the windshield column, so this may be an addition by a later civilian owner, or a post-1950 field modification. **Bottom right:** Similarly, a flexible spotlight has been added to the left windshield column of an M5A1.

Top left: The driver's position in the M5A1 was reasonably spacious. The instrument panel and the arrangement of the foot pedals was the same as on the M5. On top of each of the steering brake levers were two thumb-operated buttons, for locking the steering brakes and actuating the horn and the trailer brakes. The vertical housing to the far right contained a fire extinguisher. **Top right:** The permanently installed metal canopy frame of the M5A1 was durable enough to support a ring mount and .50-caliber machine gun. Here, the canvas top is in place and the underside of the ring mount is visible. **Bottom left:** Web straps pass through the canopy frame and are fastened to buckles inside the cab, to secure the canvas top. An electric windshield wiper was located at the top of the windshield. **Bottom right:** Below the transmission gearshift lever of the M5A1 is the fuel tank selector valve. To the right of the valve, below the driver's seat, are the choke hand lever and fan clutch hand lever.

Top left: The M5A1 provided for five passenger seats behind the front seats, facing aft. Similar to the M5, two folded blankets and a rubber pad were inserted in the seat cushion envelopes of the M5A1. Under the seat cushions in the M5A1 were doors providing access to mechanical components. Behind the seat backs were small storage compartments. **Top right:** In this view of the rear of the cab of an M5A1 are the two shell boxes, between which are two seats, piled with boxes and equipment. The permanent rear three-pane windshield and heater are non-standard additions. **Bottom left:** Five-gallon cans are stored in the left-hand shell box. The wire grille appears to have been another later modification. **Bottom right:** This view of the underside of an M5A1's top and canopy, facing toward the front of the vehicle, gives a good conception of how the top was secured to the canopy with web straps.

Top left: The rear of the M5A1 had the same general arrangement as the M5, with powder boxes on the outside, separated from the engine hood by grated radiator doors. The grating on the doors was covered with a fine screen. **Top right:** The pintle, rear towing hooks, and trailer brake couplings of an M5A1. **Bottom left:** The fine screen that covered the grating of the rear radiator doors is apparent in this photo. The engine exhaust is at the top right of the fan guard. **Bottom right:** This M5A1 is equipped with three-bar cleated T36E6 tracks.

M5A3 High Speed Tractor

Basically, the 13-ton M5A3 high-speed tractor was an M5A1 with a horizontal-volute suspension instead of vertical volute, and T82 cast-steel tracks. The center-guide, interlocking T82 tracks were 21 inches wide and were connected with straight steel pins. The prominent suspension frames of the M5A1 were absent on the M5A3. Instead, the bogies and return rollers were mounted to a less noticeable suspension frame that was attached to the sides of the hull. (U.S. Army)

The engine of this M5A3 is running, judging from the spinning fan. When M5 high-speed tractors were fitted with this suspension, they were designated the M5A2. (U.S. Army)

13 TON HIGH SPEED TRACTOR M5A3

The T22 Heavy Tractor in this photo was the prototype for a fifth-wheel version of the Allis-Chalmers-built, 38-ton M6 high-speed tractor. It was designed to tow semi-trailers carrying heavy weapons, including the 8-inch gun and 240mm howitzer. The horizontal volute suspension included three bogies on each side. Visible on the rear of the engine compartment are the two oil-bath air cleaners, the exhaust lines, and mufflers, one for each engine. (Patton Museum, Ft. Knox, KY)

The fifth wheel and retracted A-frame are evident in this photo of the T22, as is the double-drum Gar Wood 6M winch. The winch had a maximum line pull of 55,000 pounds and had direction-changing sheaves. This allowed it to pull, in addition to the rear, to the front by passing the cable under the tractor by way of rollers, as shown here. (Patton Museum, Ft. Knox, KY)

The T22 tows an M1 240mm howitzer tube in the Mack manufactured T29 semi-trailer (this was part of Mack project to tow the 240mm gun in three loads, each pulled by the Mack T16 wheeled tractor). T22 was not standardized, because the army opted instead for full-trailer carriages for the heavy weapons it was designed to transport. However, a similar prototype was standardized: the T23, which had an ammunition box in place of the T22's fifth wheel and A-frame. (Patton Museum, Ft. Knox, KY)

This page and next: The standardized M6 was designed as a prime mover for the 240mm howitzer, the 8-inch gun, and the 4.7-inch anti-aircraft gun. It had seats for ten men, including the driver, and was powered by two Waukesha 145 GZ inline six-cylinder engines, each with a minimum-rated 210 horsepower at 2,100 rpm. The horizontal volute suspension of the M6 was noticeably different in appearance from the T22's. (U.S. Army)

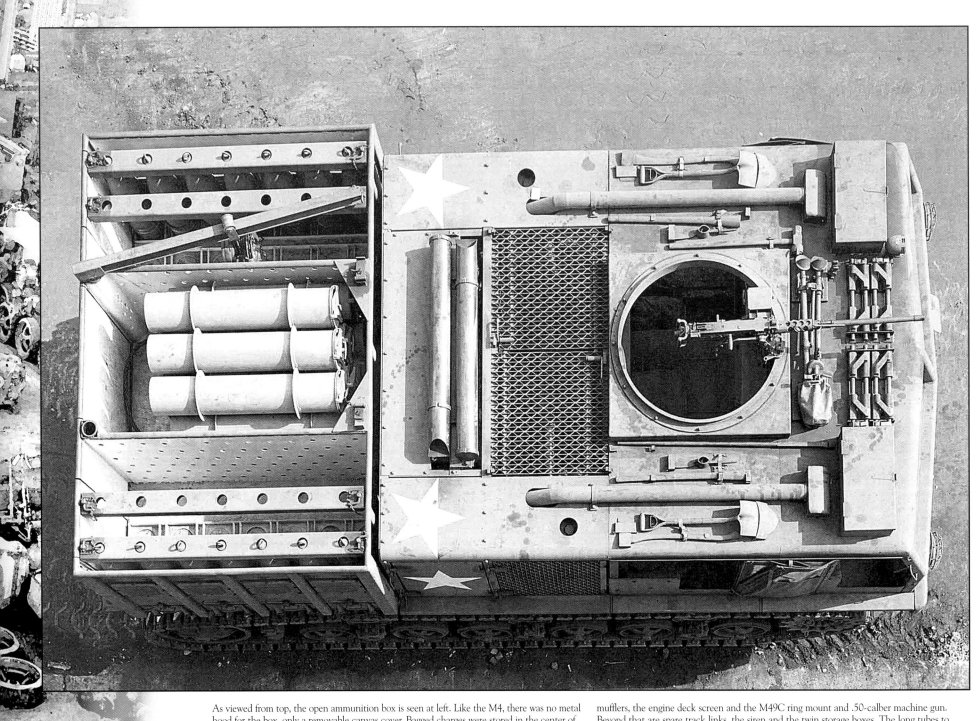

As viewed from top, the open ammunition box is seen at left. Like the M4, there was no metal hood for the box, only a removable canvas cover. Bagged charges were stored in the center of the bay, while shells were stored along the outside. A handling crane was mounted on the left side to facilitate the loading and unloading of ammunition. Continuing to the right are the mufflers, the engine deck screen and the M49C ring mount and .50-caliber machine gun. Beyond that are spare track links, the siren and the twin storage boxes. The long tubes to either side of the roof are the air intake ducts. Dual sets of pioneer tools (ax, shovel, pick head and mattock) are stowed on either side of the air cleaner tubes. (U.S. Army)

The following sequence was taken on the factory floor of Allis-Chalmers in the summer of 1945. Early in the assembly process, an M6 chassis, seen from the rear, has the winch cable rollers, trailer electric brake coupling socket (right of the roller), and taillights installed. Also in place are the towing clevises, trailer air-brake hose couplings and guards, and trailing idler arm assemblies. The rear pintle will be installed over the large circular cutout. (LaPorte County Historical Society)

Mechanics are installing the engine assembly. The differential, transmission, and final drive are already in place. This photo of the M6 before the front hull plate has been installed demonstrates how the housing of the front emplacing pintle was attached to a heavy cross member. Clearly visible are the volute springs of the bogies and the three drive sprockets per side. (LaPorte County Historical Society)

The two radiator assemblies have been installed, as well as the fan assemblies, air cleaners, exhaust lines, and mufflers. Each radiator assembly consisted of three fin-and-tube radiators housed in a single shell. The radiator toward the outside of the tractor was for cooling the torque-converter fluid, the center one was for the water in the engine cooling system, and the inner radiator was for cooling oil from the transmission, differential, and PTO cases. (LaPorte County Historical Society)

The front cowl and cab sides and canopy frame have been fitted to this M6. To the right of the radiator is the dirt receptacle of the air cleaner, and to the right of that is the rear frame of the engine compartment. (LaPorte County Historical Society)

As viewed through the rear of the engine compartment, the cylindrical air cleaners are on the outside rear of the compartment. The large-diameter exhaust ducts of the two engines connect to mufflers. As shown here, the tops of the mufflers are exposed above the roof of the M6, while the bottom halves of the mufflers are within the top of the engine compartment. The top engine grille is raised up. There was no rear cover, per se, for the engine compartment; when the ammunition box was in place, it effectively covered the opening. (LaPorte County Historical Society)

Allis-Chalmers had a large test track at its facility (inset). Each of the M6 tractors to roll off the assembly line was run 25 miles on this track, to shake out the "bugs." After delivery to Army Ordinance, the tractors were run a further 10 miles before being issued to the troops. M6's at Allis-Chalmers were delivered to the track on the back of an M26 Tank Transporter. (LaPorte County Historical Society)

After final testing, the tractors were loaded aboard railway flat cars under their own power for distribution overseas. This, in fact, was the final M6 produced by Allis-Chalmers. In the foreground are crated spare tracks, a small part of the equipment to accompany the tractor on its journey to the troops. (LaPorte County Historical Society)

An ordinance team performs maintenance on one of the mufflers of an M6 in the field. The M6 was so new at this time (October 1944) that the muffler was not yet in the logistics chain, necessitating fabrication of this part. The markings on the front of the tractor are mud spattered. On the cowl are two small, shuttered cab vents to the right of the star, and a large cab vent with a grille. The two tool boxes, a horn and siren are all visible on the roof of the cab. (NARA)

An M6 tows a 240mm howitzer tube dubbed *Berlin Bound III*. The ammunition box of the M6 had five stowage compartments. Two compartments on the upper sides of the box held shells. An inner compartment fitted with a swivel crane with a trolley hoist contained powder charges, or dunnage. The lower right compartment with the four small doors, as seen here, was for carrying water cans. A similar compartment with four small doors on the other side of the tractor was for storing tow chains, snatch block and oil. (NARA)

High speed, indeed! This M6 is towing a 240mm howitzer tube at, or near, its top speed of 20 mph. Notice the spare tire under the ammunition box cover. (NARA)

This M6 is pulling a very unusual load at the PAC Combat Training center on Oahu. This 240mm howitzer carriage is mounted on a pair of tracked transport wagons. In their prototype stage, both were designated T17E1. The combination was later standardized as either the M1E1 or M1E2, depending on the version of the gun being towed (1 for the 240mm and 2 for the 8-inch gun). These did not enter service in time for deployment in the ETO, but were seen in the final stages of the pacific campaign. (Patton Museum, Ft. Knox, KY)

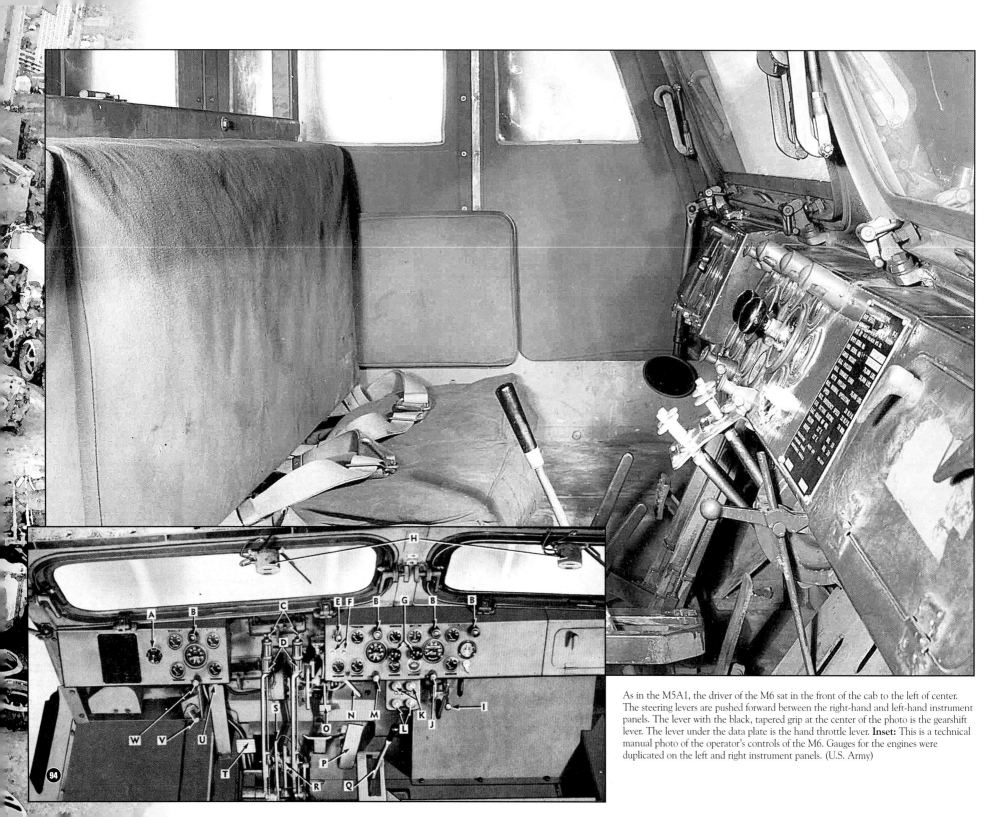

As in the M5A1, the driver of the M6 sat in the front of the cab to the left of center. The steering levers are pushed forward between the right-hand and left-hand instrument panels. The lever with the black, tapered grip at the center of the photo is the gearshift lever. The lever under the data plate is the hand throttle lever. **Inset:** This is a technical manual photo of the operator's controls of the M6. Gauges for the engines were duplicated on the left and right instrument panels. (U.S. Army)

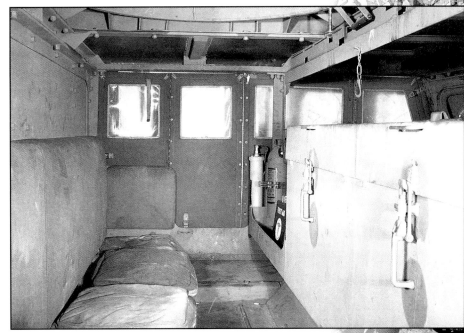

Top left: Below the right-hand instrument panel of the M6 is a small console with the engine ignition switches (top) and choke controls (bottom). To the right of the console is the hand throttle lever, used to regulate the speed of the engines during warming up or idling. **Top right:** A universal rifle bracket, holding, in this case, an M1 Garand rifle, is mounted above the windshield. **Bottom left:** A compass is mounted on the lower part of the center windshield column. This was a common post-war addition. **Bottom right:** The rear compartment of the M6 cab had seats for five, facing toward the front of the tractor. To the right are two storage boxes and a recess for fire extinguishers. (George C. Marshall Museum, Overloon, Netherlands)

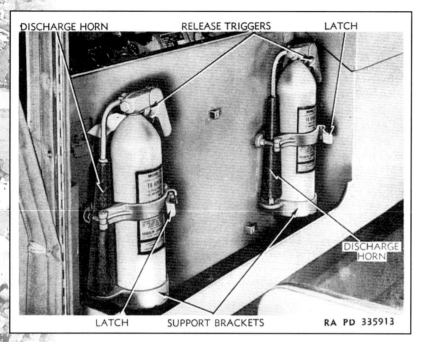

DISCHARGE HORN RELEASE TRIGGERS LATCH

DISCHARGE HORN

LATCH SUPPORT BRACKETS

RA PD 335913

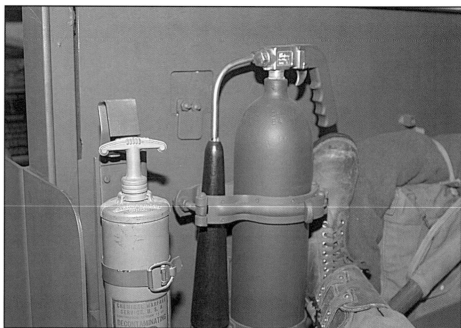

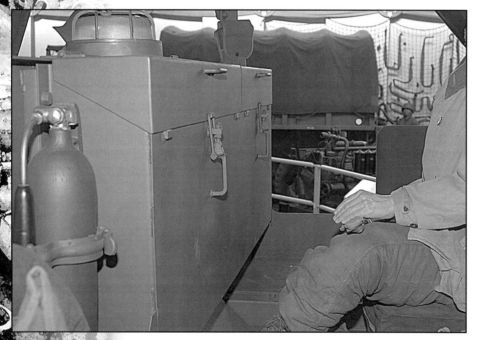

Top left: A photo from the M6 tech manual shows how the four-pound CO_2 fire extinguishers were stored in a recess behind the front left seat. **Top right:** In this restored M6, a chemical warfare decontaminator and a fire extinguisher are stowed in the fire extinguisher compartment. Decontaminators had to be recharged every three months, as the contents deteriorated quickly. **Bottom left:** A view through the rear compartment of the cab of an M6 from the right side of the vehicle. The lamp seen on top of the box was added by the museum to illuminate the interior of the tractor. **Bottom right:** The framing of the canopy of the M6 is apparent in this view. (George C. Marshall Museum, Overloon, Netherlands)

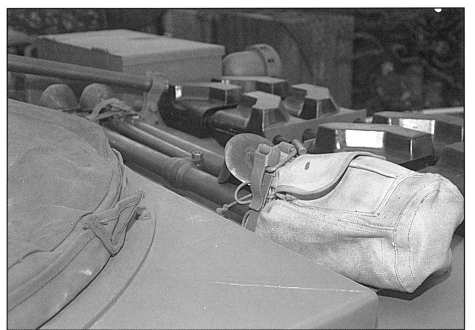

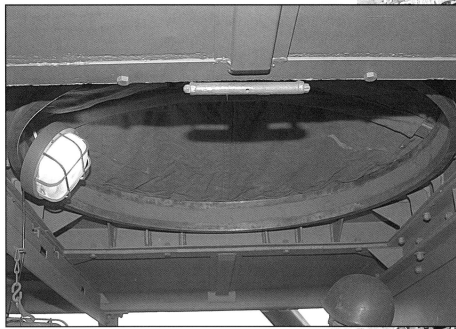

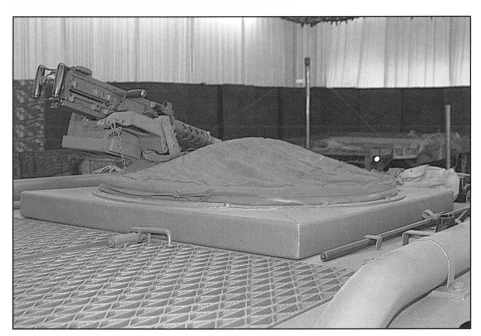

Top left: As viewed across the roof of an M6 toward the front left of the vehicle, the base of the machine gun ring with canvas cover is at left. In front of it is a machine gun tripod, beyond that are spare track links, the siren and storage box. **Top right:** In this view of the underside of the M49C machine gun ring mount, the bow supporting the canvas cover is visible. **Bottom left:** Looking forward over the top engine grille, the right air intake duct is at the far right. The canvas cover of the ring mount had a small cutout on the edge to accommodate the machine gun carriage. **Bottom right:** The air intake duct feeds into the air intake, the small box to the rear of the larger storage box near the front of the cab top. An identical air intake duct and air intake was on the opposite side of the M6. (George C. Marshall Museum, Overloon, Netherlands)

Left: The bogies of the M6 were of horizontal volute design. The cast-in markings of the seat for the volute spring are clearly visible in this photograph. Molding marks are apparent on the rubber tires of the bogie wheels. The return rollers, also called track support rollers, are of all-steel construction and are mounted in pairs on shafts bolted to brackets on the sides of the hull. **Top right:** A side view of a bogie assembly and return roller of an M6. Each track was composed of 83 blocks, linked by end connectors with wedge bolts. The center guides, or horns, were two-pronged, and attached to the tracks with bolt-on guide caps. (U.S. Army) **Bottom right:** A close-up view of an end connector and return roller, with details of the inner side of the track. (Left and above, George C. Marshall Museum, Overloon, Netherlands)

Top left: The open doors of the left side of an M6 ammunition box reveal five-gallon cans. In service, these compartments generally held a snatch block, oilcans, and tow chains. (U.S. Army) **Top right:** The rear of the ammunition box of the M6 had three large, bottom-hinged doors with chain stays. A smaller, side-hinged door was provided for the rear of the lower left compartment, but not for the right. The fuel filler pipe is to the right of the winch cable rollers. **Bottom left:** This view of the right rear side of the ammunition box shows thee side vents and lower compartment doors. The ammunition box could be slid back on its mounting, enabling better access to the engines, or it could be completely removed with the help of an A-frame and chain hoist. (George C. Marshall Museum, Overloon, Netherlands) On the M6, the volute springs of the trailing idler assemblies are housed inside the hull. The springs operate against the idler arm by way of a shaft that passes through the side of the hull and connects to a spring arm. The bottom compartment of the right side of the ammunition box was for the storage of water cans, and normally the snatch block, seen here, was stored in the compartment on the other side of the vehicle. (U.S. Army)

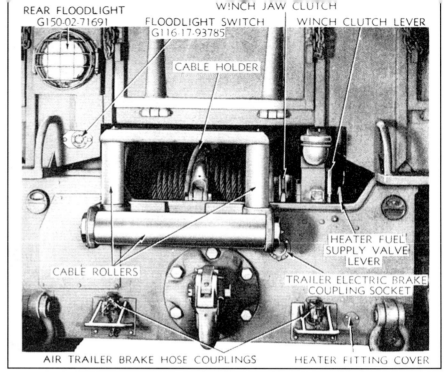

REAR FLOODLIGHT
G150-02-71691

WINCH JAW CLUTCH

FLOODLIGHT SWITCH
G116-17-93785

WINCH CLUTCH LEVER

CABLE HOLDER

HEATER FUEL
SUPPLY VALVE
LEVER

CABLE ROLLERS

TRAILER ELECTRIC BRAKE
COUPLING SOCKET

AIR TRAILER BRAKE HOSE COUPLINGS

HEATER FITTING COVER

Left: A detail of the rear 12-volt floodlight of an M6. Bolts on either side secured the floodlight guard. The floodlight switch is out of view in this photo, behind the winch cable roller at bottom right. **Top right:** A tech manual photo of the lower rear end of the M6 calls out the various components. **Bottom right:** The emergency and service air brake lines of the towed vehicle are connected to the hose couplings. To the right of the winch cable roller, an electric cable has been plugged into the trailer electric brake socket. The panel below the left of the roller provides access to the winch brake. (George C. Marshall Museum, Overloon, Netherlands)

Three pilot vehicles for the T43E1 cargo tractor were built in 1949. The third vehicle appears in this view. The tractor was designed to tow loads as heavy as the 155mm howitzer and shared components with the M24 Light Tank. A Continental AO-895-w six-cylinder, 375-horsepower engine powered it through an Allison CD-500-2 cross-drive transmission. The engine was housed under the two-seat cab. (NARA)

An M8E2 undergoes climbing trials at the Allis-Chalmers test track. The tractor could climb a 60 percent grade. The suspension was torsion bar, with shock absorbers on the two front and two rear bogies, and bumper springs for all six bogies on each side of the vehicle. The winch was at the rear of the vehicle, with an access door above the pintle. The winch controls can be seen at the top left of the rear of the cab. (LaPorte County Historical Society)

The M8E1 cargo tractor was a development of the T42 cargo tractor, standardized as the M8 in 1945. It featured two one-man cabs distinguished from the later M8A1 by their sloping windshields. The right cab was topped with an M68 ring mount for a .50-caliber machine gun, the cradle and ammunition tray of which are seen above the canvas cover. (APG)

U.S.A.
40226904

Authorized for production in July 1950, the Allis-Chalmers M8E2 cargo tractor was later standardized as the M8A1 cargo tractor. On the left side of the cowl are hydraulic lines for operating a bulldozer blade. (A cover was available for covering these lines and fittings.) Mounted on the cargo platform behind the cab is the T48 body kit for use when the tractor is towing the 75mm T69 Skysweeper antiaircraft gun. This kit contained gates, seats for nine-man gun crew, radio and ammunition boxes, and, at the rear, a frame and hoist for the large M18 generator that powered the gun's systems. (APG)

An accessory for the M8A1 was the T84E4 bulldozer blade. It was used for clearing earth for gun emplacements. The manual for the tractor cautioned against excessive use of the bulldozer; the vehicle's systems weren't built for heavy 'dozing. The pipe projecting from the cab top is the exhaust. This tractor is fitted with sand shields, which ran the full length of the fenders and were made of rubberized fabric and metal brackets. (NARA)

This M8 is seen on maneuvers in Louisiana on November 2, 1955. This shot provides a clear view of the bulldozer blade, or as it was more correctly known: the bulldozer mud board. The actual blade was considered to be the very bottom of the unit and this portion was both reversible and interchangeable. (NARA)

Also deployed for peacetime maneuvers, this time in April of 1957, this M8 has it full Body Kit Paulin in place. This covered the entire cargo bed, but not the generator hoist lifting arms on those vehicles equipped with the T48 cargo bed. Visible to the rear of the open cab compartment door is the Engine Air Cleaner Access Door. (NARA)

U.S. ARMY
11A 510

Another view of the same tractor as the previous page. Two hydraulic cylinders project vertically above the T84E4 blade when fully lowered, but the mud board in this view blocks them. The pioneer tool rack on the front of the hull is empty. The cover on the vertical plate between the two cabs is the personnel heater access cover. On the deck in front of that plate is the engine air inlet grille. (NARA)

The M8 is seen racing down a road during Exercise Great Bear, held in Alaska in February of 1962. This tractor, like the one on the previous page has a supplementary exhaust stack in place. This simple sheet metal appliance redirected the engine exhaust and helped to shield the large screened area below it. The base of the unit extended across the entire screened area. (NARA)

Speeding along in, perhaps, its ideal environment is this M8 of D Company, 4th Brigade, 23rd Infantry Division. The entire tractor has been painted white for Exercise Timber Line held at Fort Richardson Alaska in February of 1963. The stenciled triangle marks it as an "aggressor" force vehicle. Note the installed radio equipment. (NARA)

Troops of the same unit take advantage of somewhat nicer weather to conduct engine maintenance on their M8. The power plant was mounted on rails that traversed over rollers on the floor of the engine compartment. To access the power plant, it was only necessary to open the hull front door and pull out the unit. This shot also provides an excellent perspective of the entire supplementary exhaust stack and its screen. (NARA)

In addition to the T48 and the regular cargo body, other experimental bodies were utilized with the basic M8 chassis. This arrangement was termed the M62 wrecker (not to be confused with the wheeled M62 wrecker) and it consisted of an articulated boom with an enclosed cab for the operator. The inset shows the unit being used to recover an M113. Both photos were also taken in Alaska during exercise Great Bear in 1962. Note the sheet metal "hat" added to the supplementary exhaust stack, a further measure to prevent moisture from entering this area. (NARA)